FARGO PUBLIC LIBRARY

What Animal Has These Parts?
FEET

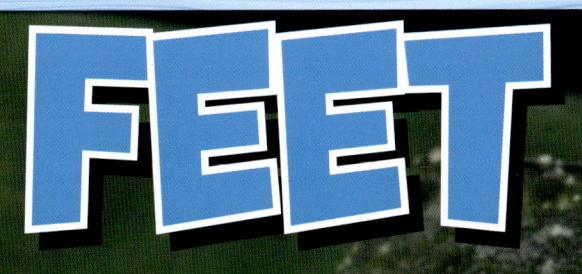

AMY CULLIFORD

A Crabtree Roots Book

CRABTREE
Publishing Company
www.crabtreebooks.com

School-to-Home Support for Caregivers and Teachers

This book helps children grow by letting them practice reading. Here are a few guiding questions to help the reader with building his or her comprehension skills. Possible answers appear here in red.

Before Reading:
- What do I think this book is about?
  - *I think this book is about feet.*
  - *I think this book is about animals that have feet.*
- What do I want to learn about this topic?
  - *I want to learn what different animal footprints look like.*
  - *I want to learn which animal has the smallest feet in the world.*

During Reading:
- I wonder why…
  - *I wonder why bears have really big feet.*
  - *I wonder why some animals have hooves.*
- What have I learned so far?
  - *I have learned that animal feet can be big or small.*
  - *I have learned that animal feet have different shapes.*

After Reading:
- What details did I learn about this topic?
  - *I have learned that feet help animals walk and run.*
  - *I have learned that feet can have claws, hooves, or webbed toes.*
- Read the book again and look for the vocabulary words.
  - *I see the word **hooves** on page 7 and the word **horse** on page 8. The other vocabulary words are found on page 14.*

What **animal** has big **feet** like this?

A **bear!**

5

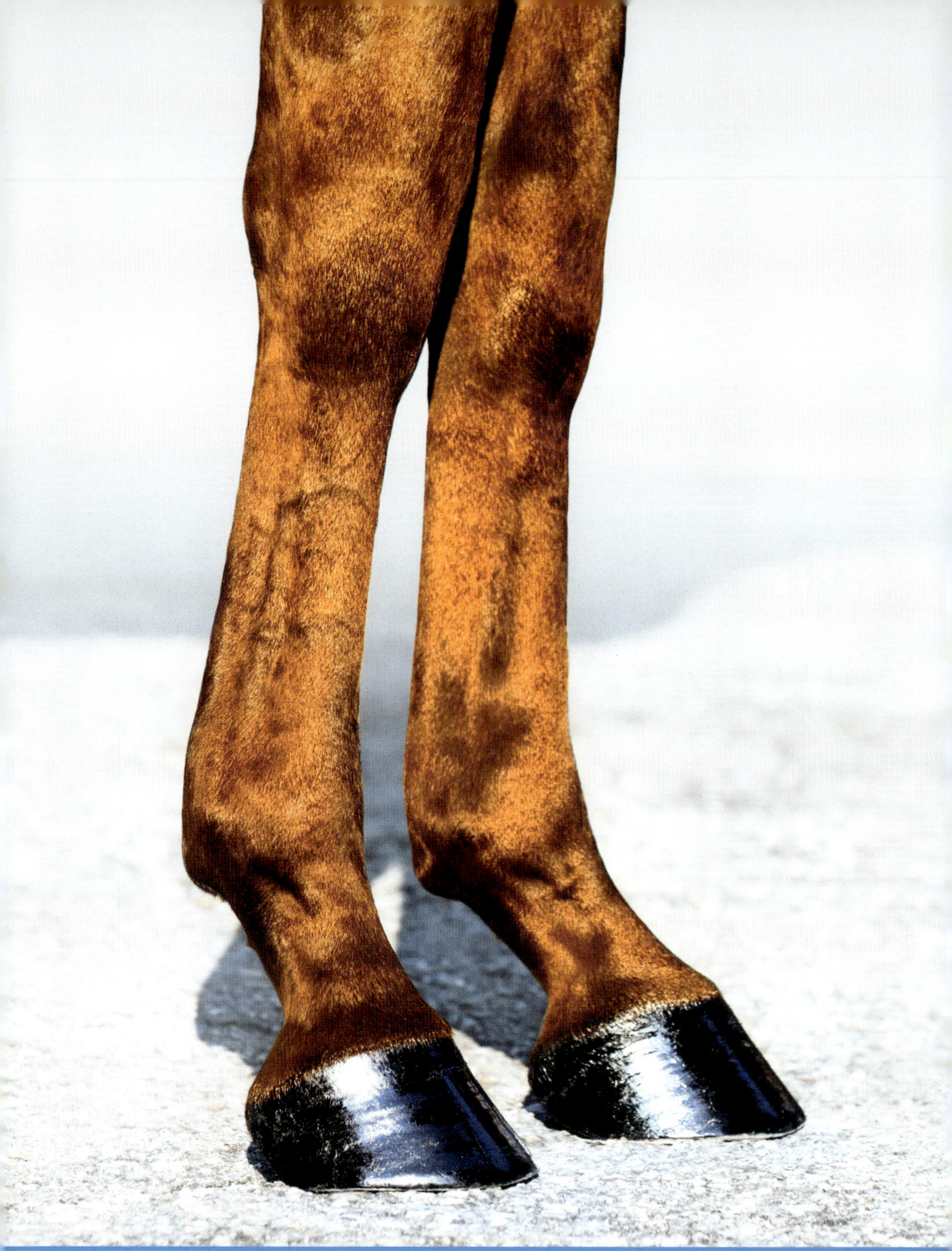

Which animal has feet with **hooves** like this?

A **horse!**

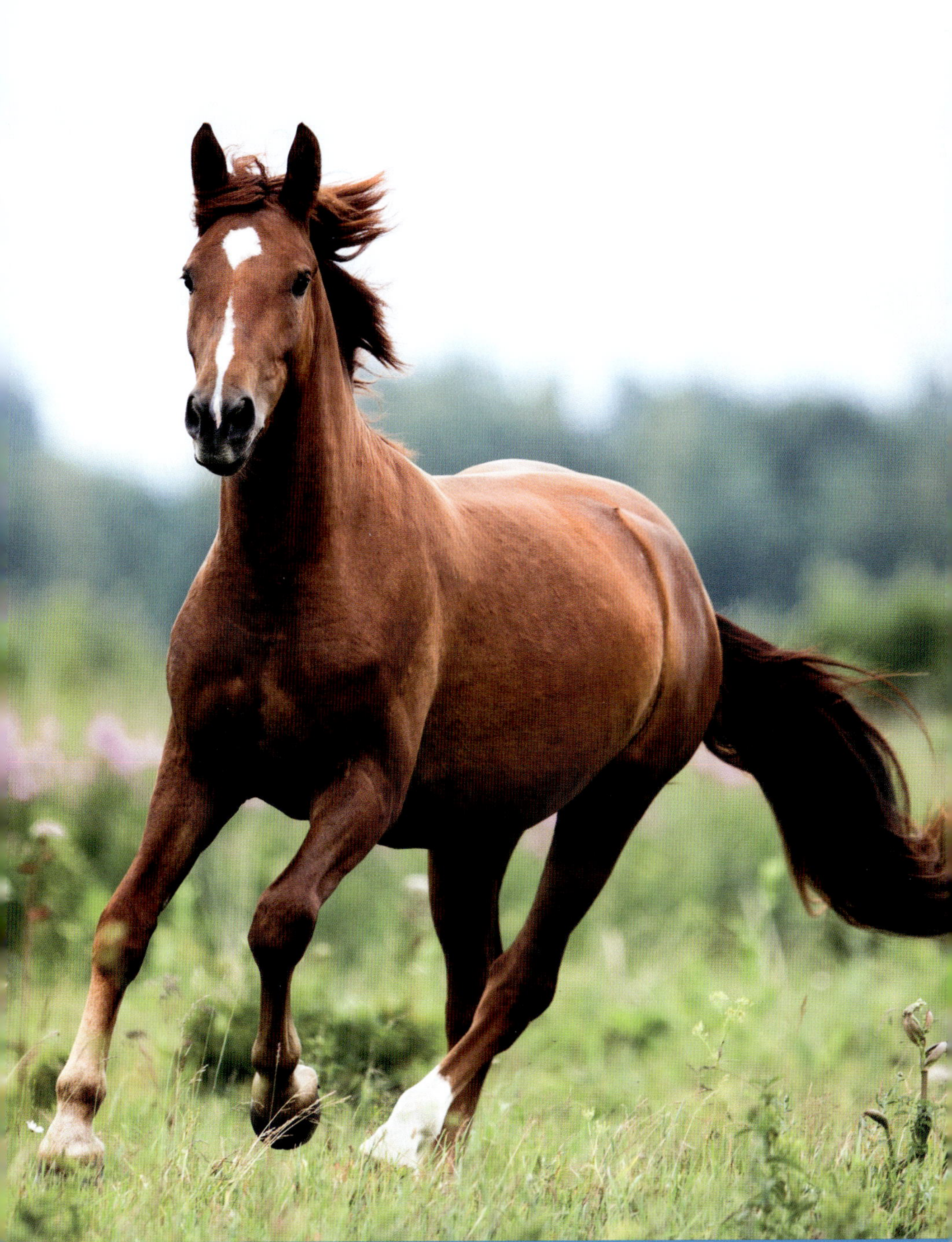

What animal has **webbed** feet like this?

11

A **frog!**

13

Word List

Sight Words

a	like	which
big	this	with
has	what	

Words to Know

animal    bear 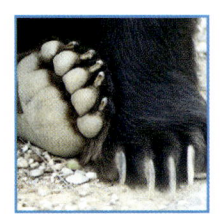   feet

frog 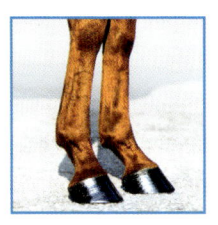   hooves    horse    webbed

28 Words

What **animal** has big **feet** like this?

A **bear**!

Which animal has feet with **hooves** like this?

A **horse**!

What animal has **webbed** feet like this?

A **frog**!

What Animal Has These Parts? FEET

Written by: Amy Culliford
Designed by: Bobbie Houser
Series Development: James Earley
Proofreader: Janine Deschenes
Educational Consultant: Marie Lemke M.Ed.

Photographs:
Shutterstock: Perpis: cover; reptiles4all: p. 1; Unfiltered Adventures: p. 3, 14; Michael Stokes: p. 5, 14; Alexia Khruscheva: p. 6, 14; OlesyaNickolaeva: p. 8-9, 14; Dr Morley Read: p. 11, 14; Ilias Strachinis: p. 13-14

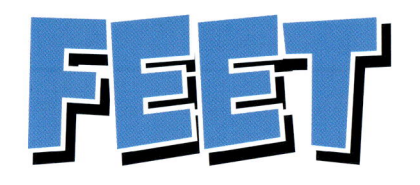

Library and Archives Canada Cataloguing in Publication

CIP available at Library and Archives Canada

Library of Congress Cataloging-in-Publication Data

CIP available at Library of Congress

Crabtree Publishing Company

www.crabtreebooks.com   1-800-387-7650

Copyright © 2022 **CRABTREE PUBLISHING COMPANY**   Printed in the U.S.A./CG20210915/012022

All rights reserved. No part of this publication may be reproduced, stored in a retrieval system or be transmitted in any form or by any means, electronic, mechanical, photocopying, recording, or otherwise, without the prior written permission of Crabtree Publishing Company. In Canada: We acknowledge the financial support of the Government of Canada through the Canada Book Fund for our publishing activities.

Published in the United States
Crabtree Publishing
347 Fifth Avenue, Suite 1402-145
New York, NY, 10016

Published in Canada
Crabtree Publishing
616 Welland Ave.
St. Catharines, ON, L2M 5V6